Ken Griffey, Jr.

Additional Titles in the Sports Reports *Series*

Andre Agassi
Star Tennis Player
(0-89490-798-0)

Cal Ripken, Jr.
Star Shortstop
(0-89490-485-X)

Troy Aikman
Star Quarterback
(0-89490-927-4)

David Robinson
Star Center
(0-89490-483-3)

Charles Barkley
Star Forward
(0-89490-655-0)

Barry Sanders
Star Running Back
(0-89490-484-1)

Michael Jordan
Star Guard
(0-89490-482-5)

Deion Sanders
Star Athlete
(0-89490-652-6)

Jim Kelly
Star Quarterback
(0-89490-446-9)

Junior Seau
Star Linebacker
(0-89490-800-6)

Mark Messier
Star Center
(0-89490-801-4)

Emmitt Smith
Star Running Back
(0-89490-653-4)

Chris Mullin
Star Forward
(0-89490-486-8)

Frank Thomas
Star First Baseman
(0-89490-659-3)

Hakeem Olajuwon
Star Center
(0-89490-803-0)

Thurman Thomas
Star Running Back
(0-89490-445-0)

Shaquille O'Neal
Star Center
(0-89490-656-9)

Chris Webber
Star Forward
(0-89490-799-9)

Steve Young
Star Quarterback
(0-89490-654-2)

SPORTS REPORTS

Ken Griffey, Jr.

Star Outfielder

Glen Macnow

Enslow Publishers, Inc.

44 Fadem Road   PO Box 38
Box 699   Aldershot
Springfield, NJ 07081   Hants GU12 6BP
USA   UK

Dedicated to Anthony "Norton" Kveragas.

Norton, old pal, you're the greatest!

Library of Congress Cataloging-in-Publication Data

Macnow, Glen.
    Ken Griffey, Jr., star outfielder / Glen Macnow.
        p. cm. — (Sports reports)
    Includes bibliographical references and index.
    Summary: Profiles the personal life and professional career of the
centerfielder for the Seattle Mariners, Ken Griffey, Jr.
    ISBN 0-89490-802-2
    1. Griffey, Ken, Jr.—Juvenile literature. 2. Baseball players—United States—
Biography—Juvenile literature. 3. Seattle Mariners (Baseball team)—Juvenile
literature. [1. Griffey, Ken, Jr. 2. Baseball players. 3. Afro-Americans—Biography.]
I. Title. II. Series.
GV865.G69M33   1997
796.357'092
[B]—DC21   96-52742
                                                                                CIP
                                                                                 AC

Printed in the United States of America

10 9 8 7 6 5 4 3 2

Illustration Credits: *The Seattle Times,* pp. 10, 15, 21, 23, 32, 34, 41, 44, 46, 53, 55, 64,
67, 71, 75, 80, 84, 87, 93.

Cover Illustration: AP/Wide World Photos.

Contents

Chapter 1

All-Around Player

Back in 1990, a man named Jim Lefebvre was the manager of the Seattle Mariners. Sitting in the dugout at Boston's Fenway Park one summer day, Lefebvre was asked for a scouting report on his center fielder. The player's name was Ken Griffey, Jr.

"Junior is gifted in so many ways," Lefebvre said. "His outfield play. His throwing. His hitting, especially his great power. He can run the bases. He can beat you every possible way."[1] Ken Griffey, Jr., was just twenty years old at the time.

The Kid, as he was called back then, grew up to prove his manager correct. By the mid 1990s, he had emerged as one of baseball's greatest players. For seven seasons in a row, fans voted him to start in the All-Star Game. The fans knew what they were doing.

Junior Griffey is the total package for a baseball player—fast, strong, smart, and dedicated to his sport.

Consider Lefebvre's high praise, word by word:

"His outfield play." Junior is an annual lock to win the Gold Glove Award, which goes to the best defensive player at each position. From his command post in center field, he takes control of the defense. He glides in or out, left or right, to track down any ball hit in the same Zip Code. Tune in baseball highlights on television any night. There is a good chance you'll see Griffey leaping high, his glove stretched over the outfield wall, to rob another hitter of a home run.

"His throwing." Laser beams seem to come from Junior's left arm. Consider one play from the 1995 American League playoffs. New York Yankees shortstop Tony Fernandez hit the ball toward the left-center-field fence. As Fernandez rounded first base, he saw Junior still chasing down the ball. Fernandez decided to stretch his hit into a double—or to try, anyway. Junior scooped up the loose ball, threw it, and cut down the startled Fernandez at second.

"That wasn't a throw, that was a cannon shot," Fernandez said after the game. "No other outfielder in baseball could have thrown me out on that play.

My mistake was not realizing who it was that I was trying to run on."[2]

"His hitting, especially his great power." Junior doesn't just hit home runs, he hits majestic rockets that seem to travel forever. He was the first player to hit the warehouse at Baltimore's Camden Yards. That was a 473-foot shot that won him the Home Run Derby at the 1993 All-Star Game. That same season, he tied a major-league record by hitting homers in eight straight games. He hit 45 homers in 1993. The next season, he led the American League with 40 homers. Do not be surprised someday, many years from now, if Griffey chases down Hank Aaron's record for career home runs.

"He can run the bases." For all his home runs, one of Junior's most famous plays is one they refer to in Seattle as the Run. It came in Game 5 of the 1995 playoffs against the Yankees. Junior was on first base, and the Mariners were down by a run, when Edgar Martinez hit the ball into the left-field corner. Junior took off like an Olympic sprinter. He ran through his coach's signal to stop at third. He looked like the fastest man on the planet sliding into home to beat the throw and win the game.

"He can beat you every possible way." In a 1996 game against the Chicago White Sox, Junior came up in the eighth inning with the score tied and

teammate Joey Cora on third base. White Sox pitcher Wilson Alvarez was afraid that Junior might win the game with a hit, so Alvarez threw the first two pitches out of the strike zone. On the third pitch, high and inside, Junior laid down a perfect bunt. It scored Cora and won the game. The White Sox were caught so off guard by the bunt that they forgot to even try to throw Griffey out at first base.

Ken Griffey, Jr., slides into home safely and scores the winning run in Game 5 of Seattle's opening round playoff series against the New York Yankees.

There are those who argue that Albert Belle of the Chicago White Sox is baseball's best player, but Belle is nothing special on defense. Some say that

Los Angeles Dodgers catcher Mike Piazza is the best, but Piazza is a slow runner. There are other great players in baseball—Jeff Bagwell of the Houston Astros, Frank Thomas of the White Sox, Mo Vaughn of the Boston Red Sox. None of those players, however, combines Junior Griffey's total package of skills.

The only all-around player who can be compared to Griffey is San Francisco Giants left fielder Barry Bonds. Like Junior, he has all the skills—speed, power, defense, hitting. But Bonds is also more than five years older than Griffey. He has reached his prime. Junior is just entering his. If you take the first seven seasons of each man's career, Junior has outhit Bonds (.302 to .274), outhomered him (189 to 176), and driven in more runs (585 to 556).

"I've been around this game forever, and this young Griffey is the best I've ever seen," twenty-two-year veteran Dave Winfield said in 1995. "It's more than his talent. There is a flair and a flash with him. That kind of player comes along once in a generation, if that often. Maybe the last one that exciting was Willie Mays."[3]

Mays stopped playing back in 1973.

Of course, the player to whom Junior is most often compared is his dad. Ken Griffey, Sr., had a nineteen-year career. It ended in 1991, but only after the Griffeys made major-league history by becoming the first father and son to play together. They were side by side in the Seattle outfield for parts of two seasons.

Because of his father's job, Junior grew up in a baseball family. He learned to hit almost as soon as he learned to walk. He went through his first season

STATS

Baseball fans like to debate who is the sport's top all-around player—Barry Bonds or Ken Griffey, Jr. Here are their statistics through the first nine years of their careers:

	Barry Bonds	Ken Griffey, Jr.
Seasons	1986–94	1989–97
Hits	1,287	1,389
Runs	890	820
Doubles	276	261
Homers	259	294
RBIs	760	872
Steals	309	123
Bat Avg.	.285	.302

in Little League without making a single out. His father was his best coach, patiently throwing him pitch after pitch before home games at Cincinnati's Riverfront Stadium. Junior spent his Easter vacations traveling to spring training to watch his dad play.

Once, when Junior was six, he got to sit in the dugout during his dad's winter ball game in Puerto Rico. When Ken Griffey, Sr., struck out the first time up, Junior said to him, "Dad, that pitcher's got nothing." Then Ken Senior struck out again the next time up. As he returned to the dugout, Junior said, "Dad, you've got nothing."[4]

Junior grew up to be the best high school baseball player in the country. In 1987, the Seattle Mariners made him the first pick in the nation in the annual draft of college and high school players. The Mariners said they hoped to see him in the majors after three seasons of minor-league ball. It took him just two seasons and 129 minor-league games to make it to the Show.

And then there's that grin. Although Junior takes his job seriously, he doesn't always look that way. He's always smiling and joking with his teammates. His cap is on backward during pregame warm-ups, because, he says, it's more fun to wear it that way. His mood is always sunny. He makes playing the game look easy.

Unlike a lot of players who make millions and seem miserable, young Griffey says, "It's never work. Work is something you have to go do and you don't want to. If you do something that's fun, you can't call it work. It's sometimes like a dream. You know, one of those dreams that are real good and you're in a deep sleep and you never really want to wake up."[5]

That bubbly personality has made Junior Griffey a favorite with fans and with advertisers. He stars in television commercials, plugging everything from sneakers to candy bars to video games. In 1994, he appeared in a movie, *Little Big League*.

On his rare days off, Junior likes to relax at home with his wife, Melissa, and their son, Trey Kenneth. There are seven dogs romping in their yard in suburban Seattle. Give Junior a sack full of cherry lollipops and sit him down in front of a video game, and he will stay happy for hours.

Of course, there is little time for those activities. Being a superstar athlete takes dedication. It means working out at the gym to improve your strength. It means hour after hour of practice to refine your skills. In 1994, the Mariners decided to offer extra batting practice to their players. The purpose was to give the club's weaker hitters a chance to catch up with the better ones, but the player who showed up

Even when Griffey is not playing he can often be seen on television in one of his many commercials. In this spot for Upper Deck trading cards he is holding Jack Corbett, a young Seattle fan.

for extra work every single day was the team's top star—Junior Griffey.

In recent seasons, he has had to be even more dedicated. In 1995, he broke his left wrist by crashing into the outfield fence while making a spectacular catch. Then, in 1996, he broke a bone in his right hand swinging the bat. Both times, doctors said he would be out for months. Both times, he worked and worked and came back earlier than expected.

If Junior can stay healthy, he can wind up as one of baseball's all-time greats. To get there, he must play another ten seasons or so. He must keep up his talent level. And he must provide more postseason heroics.

Junior has said he plans to play as long as he can—not just for himself, but for his fans as well. "You know who I play for? I play for the kids," he once said. "If there are kids out there who weren't as lucky as me and they can get some fun out of watching me play, that's great. I play to have fun and I love to see kids have fun. I love kids. I just like to see them laughing and happy, just as I always want to be."[6]

Chapter 2

Child Star

From the very start, Ken Griffey, Jr., showed signs of being a great athlete. He began walking at the age of six months, five months before most babies do. At eight months, he was already running. When he was four years old, he was whacking baseballs pitched overhand by the neighborhood teenagers.

Junior was born in 1969 in Donora, Pennsylvania, a small town near Pittsburgh. At the time, his dad was working his way up through minor-league baseball. Because minor-leaguers are not paid much money, Ken Senior took odd jobs to make ends meet. The family even received welfare checks for a time.

That all changed when Junior was four. Ken

Senior made the Cincinnati Reds as a rookie outfielder. The family (now including Junior's baby brother, Craig) moved to a nice neighborhood in suburban Cincinnati. Because Ken Senior was paid as a major-leaguer, they quickly went from being poor to being rich. It wasn't long before the other kids saw Junior being driven to his Little League games in a Rolls Royce.

Ken Senior very much wanted to be a good father. His own dad had left the family when Ken Senior was just two years old. He knew the pain of growing up fatherless, so he wanted to be more than an authority figure—he wanted to be a friend to his children. On his rare days off from baseball, there he was, pitching left-handed batting practice to the local youngsters.

"I've been hitting off him since I was real little," Junior said in 1992. "I hated for him to throw it underhand. So he pitched overhand to me. I think that's why I learned how to hit left-handers even though I hit left-handed. He'd throw me sliders, fastballs, changeups, screwballs, everything. He had pretty good stuff."[1]

Junior's mother, Alberta Griffey, was known to everyone as Bertie. She was in charge of scolding the kids when they did wrong. Sometimes she played catch, too. That ended when eight-year-old Junior threw the ball so hard that it stung her hand.

In the mid-1970s, Ken Senior was a star outfielder on the great Cincinnati team dubbed the Big Red Machine. His Reds won six division titles and two World Series in the decade. Senior did his part by hitting over .300 in three seasons and making three All-Star appearances. Junior grew up around Riverfront Stadium. He would sit on manager Sparky Anderson's lap, or horse around with the kids of other players. Soon their group became known as the Little Red Machine. At age ten, Junior often tried to stay awake at the television, watching the Reds play late-night games on the West Coast. He copied major-leaguers' batting stances—not just his dad's, but that of every member of the team.

Ken Senior told his two sons not to take baseball too seriously. For him, it was a job. For the boys, he said, it should be just for fun. But Junior always took it seriously. When he joined Little League at age nine, he went an entire season without making an out. The next season, when he struck out for the first time, he began crying. His mother tried to calm him down by reminding him that even his famous father struck out sometimes.

"I'm not my dad," Ken shouted back. "I don't make outs."[2]

FACT

Junior's Favorite Things:

Sport to watch:
Basketball

Athlete:
Deion Sanders

Food:
Lollipops

Clothes:
Jeans and sweat suits

Actor:
Danny Glover

Hobby:
Building model cars

Singer:
Bobby Brown

Athlete as a child:
Rickey Henderson

Best advice received:
"Have fun," said his dad.

Life changed for the family again in 1981 when Junior was twelve. The Reds traded Ken Senior to the New York Yankees. Rather than move the entire family across the country, Senior went by himself. He returned home during the off-season, but, for most of the time, being with Dad now meant talking to him on the phone. Once or twice a season, Junior traveled to New York to visit, but things were different than when Senior had been with the Reds. Yankee manager Billy Martin didn't like the sons of his players hanging around the locker room. Martin chased the kids off the field. He would not let them take batting practice with their dads.

Junior still had the opportunity to become close with his favorite player, Yankees outfielder Rickey Henderson. "You're going to be here in the majors someday," Henderson told Junior when he was just thirteen. "Stay away from the wrong crowd. If somebody does drugs, his name may not make the newspapers—but yours sure will."[3]

By the age of fourteen, Junior was beating his father in one-on-one basketball games. This was no ordinary dad; this was a professional athlete. At the same time, Junior started attracting major-league scouts to his baseball games. He could hit the ball four hundred feet and was the fastest runner on his team. At sixteen, he joined the Connie Mack League,

Ken Griffey, Jr., practically grew up at the ballpark. His father, Ken Griffey Sr., used to bring him to the stadium so that Griffey could meet the other pro players.

which was designed for eighteen-year-olds. His father, who rarely got to see him play, thought that Junior might not be ready for the competition. But his mother, who watched him every day, knew better. Bertie was Junior's best scout. And she was not surprised when Junior dazzled the fans during one 1986 Connie Mack World Series game by hitting three home runs—one to left, one to center, and one to right.

Like many teens, Junior became obsessed with sports. When he wasn't playing baseball, football, or basketball, he worked at a local sports arena. His job was taking tickets and cleaning up. He was also popular with the other kids. Only one thing suffered—his schoolwork.

Junior's grades at Moeller High School were so poor that he was not allowed to play on the varsity teams during the ninth or tenth grade. This frustrated him. He went to the games and enjoyed watching his friends, but he chafed at the knowledge that he was capable of being the best player on the team.

Finally, Ken Senior pulled the boy aside one day. "Do you want to make something of yourself?" Senior asked his son. "Or do you want to end up like some of these kids who won't get a job and will end up living at home with their parents?"[4]

Junior took the advice. He started studying and

improved his grades. In his junior year, he was allowed to play on the football and baseball teams. The timing was perfect in another way. That year, he grew four inches and added forty pounds to his skinny frame. He now stood 6 feet 3 inches and weighed 185 pounds.

At first, he was a football star at Moeller High. He was the punter, placekicker, and wide receiver on the football team. Colleges began sending scouts to his game, and the University of Oklahoma even

Being a tremendous athlete is one trait that seems to run throughout the Griffey family. Most people are familiar with Ken, Sr., (left) and Ken, Jr. (center), but his brother Craig Griffey is also an outfielder in the Mariners' organization.

offered him a scholarship. Years later, his younger brother, Craig, would play college football at Ohio State University.

After one season, however, Junior decided to quit football. There were two reasons. First, he did not enjoy getting hit by tacklers. Second, he believed that he was like his dad, and his best sport was baseball.

Moeller baseball coach Mike Cameron had heard rumors of how talented the young Griffey boy was, so he was excited on the spring afternoon in 1986 when Junior finally showed up to try out for the team. But something was wrong. Junior swung at the first ten pitches in batting practice, and he didn't touch a single one.

"I told him, 'That's terrible. You missed every pitch. That swing will have to go,'" Coach Cameron recalled. But Junior would not hear of making changes. "No way," he told the coach. "That's the Griffey swing."[5]

The swing stayed, and, soon enough, he began connecting. As a junior, he hit a superb .478 with 10 homers in twenty-eight games. His batting average probably would have been higher, but pitchers who knew about Griffey avoided the strike zone. They threw the ball at his shoes or two feet outside. Often, Junior chased the bad pitches out of frustration. One time, the team traveled to Dayton, about fifty miles away, where the other team didn't know who he was. The opposing pitcher threw him strikes, and Junior responded with 3 home runs. One of them flew out of the stadium and cleared a nearby building. Witnesses claim it landed five hundred feet away.

Junior's bad games only seemed to occur on those rare days when his dad was in the stands. He pressed too hard. A knot developed in his throat. He tried to hit a homer every time up, which, of course, led to his striking out. "When Dad was there, it was the only time I thought I had to impress somebody," Junior said. "He would say he was the one guy I didn't have to impress."[6]

Perhaps luckily, Ken Senior did not get to too many games. In his final high school season, Junior hit .474 with 7 home runs with 28 runs batted in and 13 stolen bases in twenty-four games. Major-league scouts came to all his games. Atlanta Braves scout Bobby Cox, who would later become the Braves' manager, called Griffey the best high school player he had ever seen. Seattle Mariners scouting director Roger Jongewaard sent his five best men out to grade Junior's talents. In their system, any player getting a score over 50 was considered a future major-league All-Star. The five scouts gave Junior scores ranging from 63 to 73.

Each June, major-league baseball teams hold a draft to select the best amateur talent in the nation. Most of those picked are college players in their early twenties. Graduating high school players may also be drafted, but they usually don't get picked early because they are young and less experienced than the college players. The 1987 baseball draft was considered one of the best in years. Two college pitchers—Jack McDowell and Mike Mussina—figured to get chosen quickly. Both went on to become big-league stars.

But neither was the first pick. That picked belonged to the Mariners, and the honor went to seventeen-year-old Ken Griffey, Jr., of Moeller High School in Cincinnati. Junior got a $160,000 signing bonus, part of which he spent on a new BMW convertible. Within weeks of graduating from high school, he was assigned to play minor-league ball two thousand miles away from home, in Bellingham, Washington.

His father made a bold prediction. Junior, he said, would be in the major leagues within three years. As it turned out, it did not take that long.

Chapter 3

Minor Leagues

After he signed with the Mariners, but before he left home to play ball, Ken Griffey, Jr., received a few words of advice from his famous father. "My dad told me that as soon as I realized this was a business, not a game, I'd be fine," Junior said. "That made me very upset. I said, 'Now I can't have any fun.'"[1]

He was just two days out of high school. The Mariners assigned him to the club in Bellingham. To him, that seemed as far away as Saturn. Even as a well-paid first-draft pick, he was living no life of glamour. Rookie League baseball meant bumpy ten-hour rides through Idaho on a bus with no bathroom. Junior would try to sneak a nap by climbing up onto the overhead luggage rack. The players stayed in cheap, roach-infested motels. The living conditions were much different from his comfortable house back in Cincinnati. It was an eye-opener for this seventeen-year-old, who had never lived away from home.

Junior badly missed his mother and his girl-friend. He tried to comfort himself with expensive toys. His favorite was his fancy BMW. He fixed it up with $6,000 worth of stereo equipment, including fourteen speakers. When he stopped at a red light, people blocks away could hear the sounds of LL Cool J coming from his car.

Making things even tougher, he was one of just a handful of African-American players on the team. He lived in a city with very few other African Americans. He had a nasty run-in with the team's bus driver's son, who called him a name insulting to his race. Junior never reported the incident, but he was upset. Not long after, that boy's brother came looking for Junior with a gun.

The loneliness and confusion affected his play. He struck out in his first at-bat, swinging at a fork ball. He had never seen that pitch before. He had no hits in his first five games. His first hit, on June 17, was a home run. Overall, he was playing poorly.

His mother traveled to Bellingham to visit him. Mrs. Griffey learned that her son had been benched for breaking a team rule by staying out late at night.

The team's manager, Rick Sweet, recognized Griffey's raw talent, but he told Mrs. Griffey that Junior needed to grow up and keep his mind on the game. The young player wasn't always hustling. Twice he got picked off of first base while he was daydreaming.

Mrs. Griffey lectured her son about the need to work hard, but she understood his loneliness. She gave him a cellular phone for his car and told him to call home as often as he liked. From that point on, his monthly phone bills averaged $800.

His game improved. After his mother's visit, he hit .450 for the rest of the season. He finished the year with a .313 batting average, 14 homers, and 40 RBIs in just 178 at-bats. The managers voted him the league's top prospect in *Baseball America* magazine. As soon as the season ended, he was sent to work on his skills in the Instructional League in Arizona. Finally, in October, he returned home. He was exhausted, but he was not about to relax.

On the outside, Griffey was coping and performing. On the inside, however, he was churning. He was still just eighteen, and facing pressures beyond those most adults ever have to deal with. Coming home didn't make things easier. Junior, who wanted to be treated like a man, started fighting with his father, who still regarded him as a boy.

Ken Senior wanted his well-paid son to start paying rent to live at home, but Junior did not understand why the rules were now different for him than they were for his younger brother and sister. Ken Senior was also offering his son more advice on life and baseball than the youngster really wanted. Father and son seemed to argue every day.

"I was confused and hurting," Griffey said. "It seemed like everyone was yelling at me in baseball. Then I came home and everyone was yelling at me there. I got depressed. I got angry. I wanted to cause some hurt for others. I didn't want to live."[2]

One afternoon, Griffey was arguing with his girlfriend and her brother. He grabbed a bottle of aspirin and quickly swallowed seventy-seven tablets. Taking too much aspirin can kill a person, and that's what Junior was thinking. As the two other teens tried to stop him, Junior ran to his car and drove away. He did not get far. He stopped a few blocks away and threw up most of the pills he had swallowed.

A friend's mother then drove Junior to the hospital, where doctors pumped his stomach. His father showed up scared and angry. He started hollering at Junior. Not knowing how to stop his dad, Junior ripped from his arm a tube that was carrying medicine to his body. That ended Senior's shouting.

The incident, terrible as it was, forever changed the relationship between father and son. They began having heart-to-heart talks. Senior agreed to listen to his son. Junior opened up and shared his feelings. Since that time, they have had a solid and loving relationship.

"The aspirin thing was such a dumb thing for me to do," Griffey said a few years later. He told the story on television, hoping it would convince other teens not to try to solve their problems by killing themselves. "Don't ever try to commit suicide. I am living proof of how stupid it is."[3]

He spent the rest of that winter recovering, physically and emotionally. When it came time for the 1988 season, he was ready. He even got a last-minute pep talk from his old high school coach, Mike Cameron. "Kenny, you've got to get serious," Cameron told him. "This is a great opportunity to make a nice living."

Griffey looked as if he was listening hard to his old coach. Then he said, "I can't wait to get there. I'm going to get into a pillow fight."[4]

Okay, so he wasn't very serious, but he was quite talented. The Mariners gave their eighteen-year-old phenom 11 at-bats against real major-leaguers in spring training. He got 4 hits. It was a hint of the greatness to come. Then they sent him to start the

Griffey's youthful attitude lets everyone know that he loves the game of baseball.

season with the San Bernardino Spirit of the Class-A California League. Most of his teammates were twenty-two or twenty-three years old, but Junior did not feel out of place.

From the start of the season, his talent was obvious. He could hit like Darryl Strawberry, play the outfield like Andre Dawson, and run like Rickey Henderson. Some experts compared him with his famous father, except that Junior had much more home-run power. *Sports Illustrated* came to San Bernardino to do a story. So did ESPN. So did ABC News.

Griffey did not disappoint. In fifty-eight games, he hit .338 with 11 homers, 42 RBIs, and 32 steals. He became so popular with the hometown fans that every time he came to bat, the public address announcer would shout, "What time is it?" The crowd would shout back, "It's Griffey time."

One day, Ken Senior, who was now playing for the Atlanta Braves, drove eighty miles to see his son after playing an early game himself in Los Angeles. Senior brought gifts—two pairs of cleats, batting gloves, a new mitt, and a thirty-five-ounce bat. Of course, the greatest gift he gave his son was his talent.

Because Junior had never played well in front of his father, he was nervous. He struck out the first time up. Determined to get a hit the next time, he laid down a bunt and beat it out with his speedy

Griffey is known for his ability to reach over the fence and take away home runs from the opposing team.

legs. Senior just sat in the stands laughing. In the fifth inning, Junior, playing center field, ran back on a towering drive. He leaped, reached his glove over the fence, and pulled the ball back. It was a spectacular catch.

In the eighth inning, with the game tied, Junior swung at a chest-high fastball. He crushed it. The ball traveled 420 feet. It cleared the fence and a nearby clump of trees for a game-winning home run.

After the game, father and son went out to celebrate with a few teammates. When they were done, Senior excitedly called his wife. It was 3 A.M. in Cincinnati when she woke up to answer the phone.

"Bertie," Senior said, "I saw greatness in our son tonight. I saw him do something in every aspect of the game. It doesn't make sense for someone to have that much talent."[5]

Junior's youth still got him into occasional trouble. His manager said that he sometimes did not pay enough attention to the game. He did not study the pitchers. Sometimes he did not run out pop-ups. He was able to get by on his natural talent. That did not cost him at this level, but it would not be acceptable when he made the majors.

The problem was that Junior was still just eighteen. His teammates were several years older, and mostly more mature. Junior was still a playful kid. He saw nothing wrong with clowning around during stretching drills, and he did not think it was a big deal when he overslept and missed a team bus ride to another game. Teammates nicknamed him Hot Dog. That meant he was a bit of a showoff. Junior did not mind the name.

"One of these days he's going to have to put together the mental aspect of the game with all of that talent," said his manager, Ralph Dick. "If he does, he'll be a major league superstar. If he doesn't, he'll be just another good major league player. And we've seen a lot of those."[6]

Hot Dog or not, Junior's talent was just too good for Class-A baseball. Late in the season, the Mariners promoted him to Vermont in the Double-A Eastern League. He played seventeen games and hit .279. He showed that he could quickly adjust to a new level.

After the season, Mariners coaches discussed whether Griffey would start the 1989 season back in Vermont or with their Triple-A team in Calgary, Alberta, Canada. The Triple-A team is where young players go when they are almost ready to play in the big leagues.

Would moving him up that fast be rushing him? Some Seattle coaches thought so.

As it turned out, Junior was ready to climb the ladder a lot faster than that.

FACT

Junior chose to wear uniform number 24 because it was worn by his favorite player, Yankees outfielder Rickey Henderson. It was also the number of Hall of Famer Willie Mays, to whom Ken Griffey, Jr., is sometimes compared.

Chapter 4

Rookie Year

Before the 1989 season began, Ken Griffey, Sr., told his nineteen-year-old son to hurry up and make the major leagues. "I'm 39 years old. I can't hold on much longer," Senior said. "If we want to be the first father and son to play at the same time, you've got to do it now."[1]

Senior was just joking. He had no idea that his dream would soon come true.

The Mariners invited Junior to spring training so they could take a look at his progress. Their hope was to start him in Triple-A Calgary. If he was good enough there, perhaps he would be up in the majors by the end of the 1989 season. There was no rush. After all, he was just three months past his nineteenth birthday.

But Junior did not want to wait. From the very start of spring training, he was on fire. He got at least one hit in each of fifteen straight preseason games. He never went more than four at-bats without getting a hit. By the end of March, he was hitting .360 and playing great defense in center field.

STATS

Ken, Sr., and Ken Jr., are not the only father and son to play in the Major Leagues. They are, however, the only pair to play at the same time.

Father	Son
Sandy Alomar, Sr., 2B, 1964–78	Sandy Alomar, Jr., C, 1988–
	Roberto Alomar, 2B, 1988–
Felipe Alou, OF, 1958–74	Moises Alou, OF, 1990–
Bobby Bonds, OF, 1968–81	Barry Bonds, OF, 1986–
Bob Boone, C, 1972–90	Bret Boone, 2B, 1992–
Ken Griffey, Sr., OF, 1973–91	Ken Griffey, Jr., OF, 1989–
Randy Hundley, C, 1964–77	Todd Hundley, C, 1990–
Hal McRae, OF, 1968–87	Brian McRae, OF, 1990–
Diego Segui, P, 1962–77	David Segui, 1B, 1990–
Mel Stottlemyre, P, 1964–74	Todd Stottlemyre, P, 1988–

On March 30, Seattle manager Jim Lefebvre called Griffey into his office for a talk. Junior expected that he was about to be sent to the minors. But the manager had something else in mind. He told Junior that he had earned a spot on the Mariners. Lefebvre said that he hoped that Junior would play center field for the team, not just in 1989, but for the next twenty years.

When Junior heard the news, he said, "My heart started beating again. They were the best words I had ever heard." Asked his goals for 1989, he blurted out, "Rookie of the Year. I want to make the All-Star team, be the MVP of the All-Star Game, win the pennant and be the MVP of the playoffs and World Series."[2] There's nothing like having high expectations!

Baseball's youngest major-leaguer called his dad to tell him that the dream had come true; they would play in the majors at the same time. No father and son had ever done that in baseball's history. When Ken Senior heard the news, he was speechless on the phone for nearly ten minutes.

Junior's mom helped him set up. She drove his car to Seattle, helped him find an apartment, and bought him clothes. Because the Mariners had a rule against player's wearing jeans or sneakers on road trips, Mrs. Griffey bought him suits, dress pants, sweaters, and fancy shoes. She hired an accountant to keep track of his money. And she made Junior promise to send home one of his two monthly paychecks. That money would go into a savings account for the future.

Because of their unique place in history, it was only natural to compare father and son. Ken Senior was a quiet player. He played a smart game, not a flashy game. In his prime, he was a great defensive outfielder and base stealer, but he was never a home-run threat.

Junior is three inches taller and twenty-five pounds heavier than his dad. That size helps make him more of a power hitter, and the way he runs and catches the ball gives him more fan flair. Some fans have called him a hot dog. Others have compared his grace and style with that of the great Willie Mays.

As people, father and son are quite different. Senior is quiet and private. Junior is more like his mom, talkative and outgoing. He is not the kind of person who ever fits into the background.

Indeed, Junior made the headlines in his first major-league game. It came on April 3, 1989, against the Oakland A's in Oakland, California. In his first at-bat, against A's star pitcher, Dave Stewart, Griffey smashed the second pitch off the center-field wall for a double. Later in the game, he also walked,

Sliding across the turf, Griffey shows the umpire that he has the ball. Because of his speed, Ken Griffey, Jr., is able to get to many balls that other outfielders would have to let fall in for hits.

scored a run, and made a great running catch of a Jose Canseco line drive.

Afterward, Griffey told reporters that he had a one-way conversation with his dad when he was standing on second base after the double. "When I got that hit," he said, "I kind of looked around and said, 'So this is what it's like?' I knew he couldn't hear me, but it was fun."[3]

Other players and managers had high praise for baseball's youngest major-leaguer. Oakland manager Tony LaRussa said, "Every time he came up tonight, I was scared. But he will be tested. It will not be a day at the beach."[4]

LaRussa was sure correct. After his double, Junior failed to get a hit in his next eighteen at-bats. People wondered how the youngster would handle his first big slump. Griffey asked advice from his father and his teammates. They all told him to just keep swinging away. Finally, he snapped out of his slump in a big way. He hit a home run on the first pitch in his first at-bat at Seattle's Kingdome. It came on April 10, his dad's birthday. After the game, Junior called Senior and said that the homer was his birthday present.

"You're not getting away that cheap." Senior laughed. "Send me a present through the mail."[5]

Junior also homered in his first at-bat the

following night, sending him on his way to an 18-for-45 stretch. Quickly his batting average climbed from .056 to .302.

Already fans could see the promise. Junior's first great game came on April 26 in the Kingdome, against the Toronto Blue Jays. In the first inning, he lined a Dave Steib slider off the right-field wall for a two-run single. In the third, he smashed another Steib pitch into the right-field corner for a double. In the fifth, he slapped a fastball over the second baseman's head for a single that started a two-run rally. Then, in the seventh, he lashed a fastball from left-hander David Wells into the seats for his third home run of the season.

Only once before in the club's thirteen-year history had a Mariner had four hits in one game. Griffey did it in the twentieth game of his career. If that was not enough, he ran down consecutive bolts by the Blue Jays' Fred McGriff and Pat Borders to the warning track in the fifth inning, eight hundred feet of outs. The first catch, which he made over his shoulder, facing the wall, was the kind that breeds legends.

It was becoming clear that Griffey and Kansas City's Bo Jackson were now the two most exciting players to watch in the American League. Griffey was just what Seattle needed. The Mariners had

Upon entering the league, Griffey, Jr., became one of the most popular players in professional baseball. The fans, young and old alike, can be seen fighting for his autograph before every game.

never had a winning season in their history. They drew fewer fans to their games than any team in the American League. Just 7,349 were on hand the night of Junior's great game against the Blue Jays. There was talk of moving the team to another city.

Junior seemed to ride to the rescue. All by himself, he was getting Seattle fans interested in baseball. The crowd would rev up as he approached the plate. Fans cheered as the public address announcer said in a low and slow voice, "Ken Grif-feeeeee Juuuuun-yer." Within months of his debut, the Mariners held a Ken Griffey, Jr., poster night. They sold Ken Griffey, Jr., T-shirts. A Seattle candy company even started selling the Ken Griffey Junior Milk Chocolate Bar. Junior said it felt great to have a candy bar named after him, even though he was allergic to chocolate.

Junior lived up to the hype. By the All-Star break in July, he had 13 homers. The most his father had ever hit in an entire season was 14. On May 31, he had his first two-homer night, against the New York Yankees. Both shots came against Yankees right-hander Jimmy Jones. The second one skyrocketed 450 feet into the upper deck at Yankee Stadium.

His defense was also superb. Junior played with a grace rarely seen in baseball. He glided after routine fly balls. When he ran full throttle after a ball in the gap, he covered more ground than any outfielder in baseball. In a game against the Boston Red Sox at Fenway Park in 1989, Wade Boggs led off the ninth with a drive to deepest center. Griffey sprinted back, leaped, twisted in the air, and caught the ball. Coming down, he slammed his head and shoulders into the fence. He lay stunned on the warning track for several seconds. Then he rolled over and held his glove aloft to the umpire to show

FACT

Ken Griffey, Jr., was one of the youngest players in major-league history to have two seasons with more than 100 RBI. Following is the list of players, with their age listed in years and months at the end of their second 100 RBI season:

Player	Age
Mel Ott	21,7
Al Kaline	21,10
Ty Cobb	21,10
Ted Williams	22,1
Joe DiMaggio	22,11
Ken Griffey, Jr.	22,11

Admiring his work, Griffey, Jr., watches the ball sail out of the yard during batting practice, prior to a big game.

he had held the ball. The Fenway fans groaned at the catch, but cheered loudly through two scoreboard replays.

It looked for sure that Junior would be the Rookie of the Year—one of his goals for the season. Then, on July 25, he slipped stepping from the shower in a hotel room in Chicago. He broke a bone in his right hand. He was on the disabled list for a month. When he returned to the lineup, he seemed to be trying too hard. He wanted to catch up for the time he missed. He wanted to finish the year with twenty homers, but he batted just .181 for the rest of the season.

"He was trying to catch up with the other Rookie of the Year candidates with one swing," said manager Lefebvre. "It wasn't surprising for a 19-year-old rookie, really. He lost his poise."[6]

Junior finished the season with 16 home runs and a .264 batting average—pretty good numbers for the youngest player in baseball. He was third in the Rookie of the Year voting, behind pitchers Gregg Olson of the Baltimore Orioles and Tom Gordon of the Kansas City Royals. The Mariners had another losing season, their thirteenth in a row. But there was a reason for hope now. Junior was a potential superstar.

Chapter 5

Like Father, Like Son

After a standout rookie season, Ken Griffey, Jr., set out in 1990 to prove he was no fluke. During the off-season he worked with weights for the first time in his life. He reported to training camp in March more muscular than he had ever been.

Any doubts that anyone might have had were soon erased. Junior was on fire at the start of his second season. At the end of April, he led the American League with a .395 batting average. He was also near the league leaders in home runs, runs batted in, hits, and runs.

Some nights, Griffey was a one-man highlight film. In an April game against the Yankees, he was in center field when New York right fielder Jesse Barfield drove the ball deep to left center field.

Junior heard the crack of the bat and raced to the outfield fence. He hit the warning track at full speed, took two giant strides, planted the cleats of his right shoe halfway up the foam padding, and leaped. His right arm cleared the eight-foot wall with room to spare. The ball disappeared over the fence as the Yankee fans cheered. But Junior pulled his glove back with the ball inside. It was an astounding catch, but not the last one he would make that season.

"The guy is playing like an eight-year veteran," Mariners manager Jim Lefebvre said. "It's amazing how he has matured so much since last year. And he's still the youngest player in the big leagues. I don't like to make comparisons, but he is a lot like Willie Mays. He's one of those rare talents that comes along once in a great while."[1]

Lefebvre gave Junior a new nickname: The Kid. It quickly stuck. And most experts in baseball agreed that if they were starting a major-league team and had the pick of any one player, it would be the Kid. He now excelled at the five skills by which complete ballplayers are measured: hitting for average, hitting for power, defense, running, and throwing. Perhaps nothing in baseball was as fun to watch as Griffey at the plate. He set his six-foot-three body upright with his hands held high and his bat cocked toward the pitcher. He has always had a beautiful swing and the rare talent of making balls soar off his bat.

Fans around baseball began to recognize this great talent. He was voted the starting center fielder for the All-Star Game. It would be his first of many appearances. At the time he was hitting .331 with 12 homers and 45 runs batted in.

Seattle fans were excited, too. Home attendance rose to a team record 1.5 million that season. Junior was so popular that security guards had to escort him through the crowds after each game. The Mariners had to limit the number of interviews and TV appearances he did.

If there was one fair knock on Junior, it was that he was no student of the game. He did not study pitchers or do his homework. Instead, he relied on his raw talent to get by. Mariners coaches worried that because success came so easily to Griffey, it might lead him into bad habits. "He's still a kid," said Mariners hitting coach Gene Clines. "This is still one big game of Whiffle Ball for him. When he finally gets serious about the game, there's no telling what kind of numbers he will put on the board. I don't think anybody's ever been that good at that age. He's just a natural."[2]

From Junior's point of view, baseball was still

one big playground. He did not want to spoil the moment by thinking like an adult. How else could he live up to that nickname, The Kid? "In hitters' meetings, I very seldom pay attention," he said. "Why think? If you go up there thinking, 'Hey, this guy has a great curve ball,' you're thinking he's going to throw a curve ball every time. Then he'll sneak a fastball by you. My approach is to look for a pitch down the middle of the plate and react to wherever it's at. I don't like to think, 'My feet are wrong, my hands are too high.' I just get up there and whatever feels comfortable, I go with it."[3]

Mostly, Mariners coaches left Junior alone, but privately, they wished he had an older role model on the team to set an example for his work habits— someone like, say, Ken Griffey, Sr.

Ken Senior started with the Reds in 1990, his eighteenth season in the majors. Cincinnati, however, had little use for a forty-year-old outfielder. By August, he was playing only as a pinch hitter and batting just .206. When the Reds decided to add another pitcher to the roster, they placed Senior on waivers. That meant they were releasing him and that any other club could claim him.

Senior had already fulfilled one dream by playing in the majors at the same time as his son. Playing on the same team together seemed too much even to hope for. Who ever imagined there might be a father-son combination on a major-league team?

The Mariners quickly said they were interested. Lefebvre said he would play the Griffeys side by side in the outfield—Ken Senior in left, Ken Junior in center. This was no publicity stunt, Lefebvre insisted. Instead, he saw the elder Griffey as the boost the Mariners might need to reach .500 for the first time in their history.

Senior had just one doubt. He worried about going to Seattle if his son was not crazy about the idea. That was Junior's territory, he thought. Maybe the twenty-year-old son would not want his father hanging around every day. "So I called him," Senior said. "I wanted to make sure that he wanted me to come out there. I got on the phone and I asked, 'Do you want me to . . . ?' And before I could even finish, he said, 'Yeah!'"[4]

The eyes of America were on Seattle on September 1, 1990. A crowd of 27,166—including Alberta Griffey—packed the Kingdome to see the Mariners take on the Kansas City Royals. Junior's brother, Craig, now a football player at Ohio State University, sent a high-tech message to the scoreboard by satellite. Ken Senior said it was the happiest day of his life. Ken Junior said it wasn't much different from playing catch with his dad in the backyard.

Before game time Griffey looks to get some fatherly advice from Ken, Sr. In 1990, the Mariners signed Ken, Sr., and started the two Griffeys side by side in the outfield.

The excitement started early. Senior, batting second in the first inning, lined a pitch from Storm Davis through the infield for a single. Junior was up next. He drilled the second pitch into right field for a single, too. The two balls were collected and sent to baseball's Hall of Fame in Cooperstown, New York. Both men then scored on a double by Mariners first baseman Alvin Davis.

As it turned out, father and son had a friendly bet. The first one to get a hit got treated to dinner. Junior said they had tied, since both singled the first time up. But Senior insisted that since he got the first hit, he had won the bet. Junior did not complain. He just paid off the bet.

At the end of that inning, father and son ran to the outfield side by side. They got a standing ovation. The Mariners won the game, 5–2. One other highlight came in the sixth inning. Ken Senior threw out Bo Jackson, probably the fastest man in baseball, trying to stretch a single into a double. He cleanly fielded the ball off the bullpen wall in left field and threw a strike to second baseman Harold Reynolds.

Afterward, Ken Senior said, "The first time up, I was really nervous. It was just like being a rookie all over again. But this is something I'm very proud of. I'm glad we're together because this is a once-in-a-lifetime opportunity for both of us."[5]

Senior's move to Seattle meant a new lease on life. In twenty-one games he hit .377—not bad for a forty-year-old. He even decided to return for the 1991 season.

Junior was energized as well. He finished the season batting an even .300. He added 22 home runs, 80 RBIs, and 16 stolen bases—not bad for a twenty-year-old.

The highlight of the season came in a late September game against the California Angels. In the fourth inning, Ken Senior walloped the first pitch thrown by right-hander Kirk McCaskill into the bleachers for a home run. Ken Junior was up

When Ken Griffey, Sr., joined the Mariners in 1990, the Griffeys became the first father and son combination to ever play for the same team. That year, in a game against the California Angels, they provided a moment that many fans will never forget when they hit back-to-back home runs.

next. McCaskill tried to slip a fastball by him. Junior turned on the pitch and drove it into the stands, not more than fifteen feet from where his father had just hit it. Back-to-back homers!

The month they spent together on the same team created a new warmth between father and son. Both enjoyed sharing their work, sharing their experiences, facing the same challenges. They were more than teammates, and they were more than relatives. They had become best friends. Senior moved into Junior's house, a turnaround from a few years earlier.

At the park, they were all business. When Ken Senior talked about opposing pitchers, Ken Junior listened carefully. Away from the park, their talks were about everything except baseball. "My son talks about cars and radios and stuff," Senior said. "I talk about, 'Don't buy it!' My boy loves to spend money as fast as he earns it. But, really, playing together is better than I ever imagined. We're finding more and more about each other. I'm finding how much he has matured, in terms of baseball and off-the-field things."[6]

The challenge now was to build a winner in Seattle. Even with the Griffeys' great seasons, the Mariners still finished in fifth place. Their 77–85 record meant they still had not had a winning season in their history. There were some talented players there, including promising pitchers Randy Johnson, Erik Hanson, and Brian Holman. Edgar Martinez and Jay Buhner looked like sluggers for the future.

What the Mariners needed was an on-field leader. Ken Griffey, Jr., knew it was time for him to accept that role.

Chapter 6

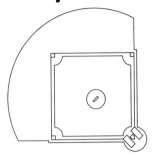

Disappointing Seasons

The Mariners' 1991 season started on a bad note. During spring training, Ken Griffey, Sr., was in a car accident. He injured his neck and back. When the season started in April, he was unable to play. He returned in May for a few at-bats, but the pain in his neck was too much. By June, he was back on the injured list after playing just thirty games. At age forty-one, he had only a slim chance for a comeback.

Nothing, it seemed, was going right for Seattle. The Mariners lost their first six games of the season. They won a few, then lost five more in a row. Without his father around, Junior fell into a slump. He batted just .226 in June—his worst month since his rookie season. At one point, he went eighteen straight at-bats without a hit. Worse, he seemed not to be hustling. In a game against the Detroit Tigers, Junior stopped running on a ground ball he hit to Alan Trammell, the Detroit shortstop. Tigers first baseman Cecil Fielder dropped Trammell's throw, which meant that Junior would have been safe—if he had run on the play.

"You're lucky that your dad didn't see you not hustling out there," Tigers manager Sparky Anderson said to Junior. Anderson had managed Ken Senior on the Reds back in the 1970s. He had bounced Junior on his lap many years ago. "People pay money to see you play," Anderson said. "You let them down."[1]

Seattle fans reacted by booing Junior for the first time in his short career, and newspaper writers got involved, too. In July, *Seattle Times* columnist Steve Kelly wrote an open letter to Junior: "We have great expectations for you," Kelly wrote. "But now we're beginning to wonder. We don't see the work habits of Willie Mays. We don't see the hunger that drove Mays into the Hall of Fame. We wonder what a player would be like with your talent and your father's hunger. Will you settle for being a multi-millionaire instead of a Hall of Famer? Maybe now it's time to go to work. It's time to be more than just a good player. It's time to be great."[2]

At first, Junior was angry about the article. Who was the writer to question him? But then he looked in the mirror and asked himself whether he was really trying his hardest. Was he dedicated enough? Was he focused on baseball? The honest answer to each question was no.

Baseball had always come easy to Junior. He had far more natural talent than did his dad, even though he never had the work ethic. Without trying very hard, he was a very good major-league player. But what would happen, he now asked himself, if he tried his hardest? How good could he be?

Junior went to work. By the end of the season, he had hit a terrific .372 with 13 home runs and 64 runs batted in. His dedication was bringing results, and the Mariners were starting to win.

By late August, the Mariners, who had never had a winning season in their first fourteen years, were leading their division for the first time ever. In an important game against the Baltimore Orioles that month, Junior displayed all of his skills. He made three outstanding catches, including a first-inning, rally-stopping, face-first catch against the center-field wall.

With the bases loaded and one out, Griffey raced straight back on a drive by Baltimore's Randy Milligan. Without breaking stride, he caught the ball at the base of the wall. Then he immediately crashed into the wall. He bounced off the padded panel, stumbled, but stayed on his feet to throw the ball back. All three runners held. The next batter flied out to end the rally.

"I was aware of the wall," said Junior. "I could see the top of it. I knew I was going to hit it. But my job is to catch the ball, isn't it? We play for the fans.

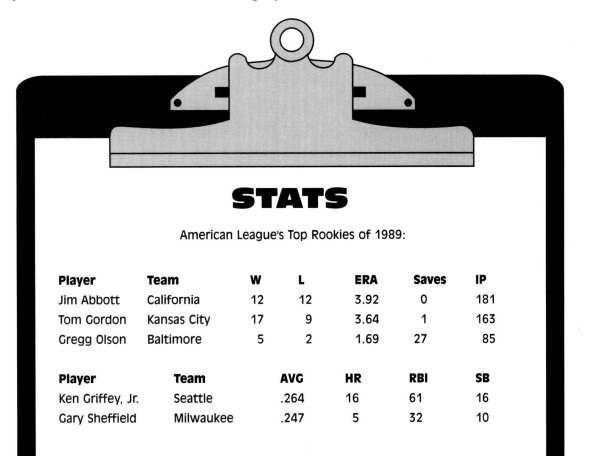

STATS

American League's Top Rookies of 1989:

Player	Team	W	L	ERA	Saves	IP
Jim Abbott	California	12	12	3.92	0	181
Tom Gordon	Kansas City	17	9	3.64	1	163
Gregg Olson	Baltimore	5	2	1.69	27	85

Player	Team	AVG	HR	RBI	SB
Ken Griffey, Jr.	Seattle	.264	16	61	16
Gary Sheffield	Milwaukee	.247	5	32	10

Without them, it wouldn't be much fun coming to the ballpark. If they're in the game, we're in the game."[3]

The Mariners did not win their division in 1991, but they did finish the season with 83 wins and 79 losses—their first-ever winning record. Junior, after looking at himself in the mirror, ended up with his best season yet. He batted .327, third best in the American League. He smacked 22 homers and 42 doubles and stole 18 bases, and he drove in 100 runs. At age twenty-one, he had reached superstar numbers.

At the end of the season, Ken Senior officially ended his nineteen-year career. He took a job as a coach and minor-league teacher with the Mariners. Senior finished his big-league career with a .296 batting average. He had 152 homers, 859 RBIs, and 200 stolen bases. He had played in three All-Star games and two World Series. The only goal he had left, Senior said, was to see his son beat all of his own numbers.

Would 1992 be the season Junior played in his first World Series? It quickly became clear that the answer was no. Although 1991 had ended well for Seattle, 1992 became a disaster.

Before the season started, the Mariners fired manager Jim Lefebvre and replaced him with Bill

Plummer. Junior had been very fond of Lefebvre, so he was disappointed. But he knew his job was to play for whoever managed the club.

Early in the season, Junior sprained his right wrist diving for a ball. He missed sixteen games. Other top Seattle players—outfielder Jay Buhner, first baseman Tino Martinez—also missed time because of injuries. By midsummer, Seattle's high hopes had died. The team fell to a 64–98 record and last place in the American League West. Manager Bill Plummer was fired after just one season.

Lost in it all was another fine season for Junior. He set personal season records for home runs (27) and runs batted in (103). He batted .308, his third straight season over .300. He also won his third straight Gold Glove Award, honoring him as the top-fielding center fielder in the league.

The highlight of 1992 came in the All-Star game at San Diego's Jack Murphy Stadium. Junior was voted a starter on the American League team for the third straight year. In the first inning, he singled in a run off Atlanta Braves pitcher Tom Glavine, to help the AL get off to a 4–0 lead. Leading off the sixth inning, he cracked a double to start another four-run rally.

Between those two at-bats, he faced Chicago

Mariners teammates Ken Griffey, Jr., and Harold Reynolds are happy to receive their Gold Glove awards.

Cubs pitcher [...] Maddux, the top pitcher in the National League [...] as the third inning. Junior sent a screaming line [...] over the left field fence for a home run. "It wa[...] of weird when I hit it. I didn't think it was go[...]ut," he said of his home run. "When it went [...] ught of my dad hitting one in 198[...] This [...] as [...] econd-biggest thrill of my career, right behind playing with my dad."[4]

In fact, his home run added to the family lore. Senior and Junior became the first father and son in baseball history both to homer in the All-Star Game. And Junior's game—3-for-3, with 2 runs and 2 RBIs—earned him the game's Most Valuable Player Award. His dad had won that honor, too, back in 1980.

Griffey enjoyed his life in Seattle. He got married that season. He and his wife, Melissa, moved into a quiet neighborhood known as Issaquah. Griffey was often seen tooling around town in one of his fancy cars, especially the one with the license plate reading THEKIDD. He made appearances on television with Arsenio Hall. He had a couple of national TV commercials and was the biggest draw at sportscard shows. Many nights, he would rent *Rocky* or *Star Wars* movies and watch them several times. He got very involved with the Make a Wish

STATS

Griffey, Jr., is among the career leaders for the best batting average in All-Star game play. Following is a list of the players with the top five All-Star game batting averages.

PLAYER	G	AB	R	H	HR	RBI	AVG
Charlie Gehringer	6	20	2	10	0	1	.500
Billy Herman	10	30	3	13	0	0	.500
Ken Griffey, Jr.	6	18	3	8	1	4	.444
Moose Skowron	5	14	1	6	0	0	.429
Steve Garvey	10	28	7	11	2	7	.395

Foundation, a charity that aims to grant wishes for sick children.

But things were far from perfect. After four seasons, he was frustrated with losing. The Mariners seemed to be going backward. He wanted to play in the World Series, as Ken Senior had, and did not see his team moving in that direction. He thought about

Ken Griffey, Jr., and his wife Melissa live in suburban Seattle with their children, Trey Kenneth (left) and Taryn.

asking to be traded to a better team. He told reporters that he had no plans to stay with the Mariners unless their front office improved the club. "We need more commitment from management to winning," he said. "I want to play in the Series, and I can't do that all by myself. I'm not knocking my teammates, but I'm tired of losing. We had it going before last season. But now, I was part of the team that just lost 98 games."[5]

He was further upset that the Mariners hired Lou Piniella as their new manager for 1993. Piniella had been manager of the Cincinnati Reds in 1990 and had feuded with Ken Senior. If Piniella was coming to Seattle, Junior said, it might be time for him to leave. His statement angered Mariners fans. They wanted him to be a team leader. Instead, he was coming off as a complainer. After reading several angry letters to the editors of local newspapers and hearing himself blasted on radio talk shows, Junior apologized to the fans.

Batting coach Gene Clines tried to explain his star player's mistakes. "Junior has to understand that he's going to be criticized," Clines said. "Everything he does is put under a microscope. But people have to realize you're still dealing with a very, very young ballplayer. Junior is still just 22. He's got a lot of growing up to do yet."[6]

In the end, the Mariners did hire Piniella as their manager for 1993. Junior and Piniella sat down and talked. They cleared up their differences. And Junior prepared himself for another season in Seattle. Maybe, he thought, just maybe, the Mariners could turn things around after all.

Chapter 7

Home Run Streak

From the start, 1993 seemed to be a new chapter in Ken Griffey, Jr.'s career. His talk with new manager Lou Piniella got him charged up about the Mariners' new direction. His dad was now his batting coach. Before the season, he signed a new four-year contract that would make him rich. And Junior decided it was time for him to become a leader.

The Kid would now be the Man.

"I'm not a teenager anymore," he said. "I'm a married man. There comes a time when you have to grow up. For me, that time is now. I'm planning on having the best season of my career."[1]

He didn't waste any time. Junior hit his first home run of the season on his first at-bat on

Opening Day. It was a three-run blast off Jack Morris of the Toronto Blue Jays. In early May, Junior socked a 460-foot homer off Scott Erickson of the Minnesota Twins. The ball hit a speaker on the Kingdome ceiling and landed in the second deck.

He had 10 home runs in the season's first two months. Junior said the big change was a better understanding of how baseball works, both mentally and physically—that, and a specially coated bat that only he, Kirby Puckett, and Barry Bonds used. Griffey's thirty-one-ounce bat was dipped twice in lacquer by the Louisville Slugger folks. As a result, the bat did not splinter as easily as others did.

Griffey, Jr., is shown here signing autographs for members of the Sakhalin Locomotives, a visiting Russian youth baseball team. A representative for the team said that Griffey is the only baseball player they had ever heard of.

Junior's home-run barrage continued. The day before the All-Star Game in Baltimore, baseball's top sluggers held a home-run derby at the Camden Yards stadium. Eight players entered and two—Junior and Juan Gonzalez of the Texas Rangers—tied for the most at the end of two rounds. In overtime, Gonzalez ripped a 455-foot shot into the upper deck. Junior came up next. He launched a ball over the right-field fence and right out of the

STATS

Junior belongs to an elite list of ballplayers who hit more than 150 home runs before the age of twenty-five.

PLAYER	HR by 25	CAREER
Eddie Mathews	190	512
Mel Ott	176	511
Jimmie Fox	174	534
Mickey Mantle	173	536
Ken Griffey, Jr.	172	—
Frank Robinson	160	586
Johnny Bench	154	389
Orlando Cepeda	154	379
Hank Aaron	140	755
Juan Gonzalez	140	—

playing area. The ball carried 473 feet until it hit the wall of a warehouse across the street. No player had ever before hit a ball off that building. Junior won the derby.

On July 20, Junior began an amazing streak. He hit a home run against Paul Gibson late in a game at Yankee Stadium. He homered in his next game against New York's Jimmy Key. In Seattle's next series at Cleveland, he hit home runs in the first two games. That meant he had homered four games in a row.

After the fourth game, Junior and his parents were eating dinner at a Cleveland restaurant. "What's the record for most games in a row with a home run?" Mrs. Griffey asked.

"Eight," said Ken Griffey, Sr. "It's held by Dale Long [Pittsburgh Pirates, 1956] and Don Mattingly [Yankees, 1987]."

"Too bad," said Alberta Griffey. "That seems impossible to reach."[2]

Mrs. Griffey underestimated her son. Junior hit home runs in two more games in Cleveland. The team returned to Seattle. In the next game, on July 27, Junior whacked a 440-foot grand slam off Kevin Tapani of the Twins. That gave him 7 homers in seven games. He was one away from tying the record.

On July 28, more than thirty thousand fans came to the Kingdome to see Junior give it a try. He struck out in the first inning. He grounded out in the fourth. The third time up, in the seventh inning, he smashed the first pitch by Minnesota's Willie Banks in the third deck in right field. He had tied the record his mother thought seemed impossible. It was his 30th home run of the year, and the fans gave him a three-minute standing ovation.

After the game, Ken Senior was asked if his son amazed him. "No, I'm not amazed," he said. "Surprised? No, I'm not surprised. I know what he can do and it's just a matter of whether he wants it. We'll see how it works out."[3]

The next night, Junior set out to break the record. The eyes of baseball were on Seattle on July 29. More than forty-five thousand fans came to the Kingdome, the biggest crowd of the year. The Twins' starting pitcher was Scott Erickson, whom Junior had always hit well. The television network ESPN cut into its broadcasts whenever Griffey came up, to show his quest for the record.

His first three at-bats produced a single, a double, and a ground out—not bad, but not what the fans were looking for. He came up in the seventh inning against Twins reliever Larry Casian. With the Mariners ahead in the game, and not likely to bat in the bottom of the ninth, this figured to be Junior's final chance.

Casian's first pitch was a curve ball that did not curve. It was the kind of pitch that Junior usually could sail into the seats, but not this time. Griffey took a big rip and popped out to second baseman Chuck Knoblauch. The streak was over. He had tied, but not broken, the record.

"I tried so hard to do it for the fans," Junior told reporters after the game. "I'll admit, I was a little

On July 28, 1993, Ken Griffey, Jr., tied a major league record held by Dale Long and Don Mattingly when he hit a home run in his 8th consecutive game. Afterwards, Ken Griffey, Sr., had a talk with his son, probably to tell him how proud he was.

nervous. I swung at some bad pitches, trying to get it out of the way. But it was fun while it lasted, wasn't it?"[4]

It sure was. So was the entire 1993 season, for that matter. Junior wound up with 45 home runs, second only to Juan Gonzalez. He led the American League in total bases. He was among the league leaders in nearly every offensive category, and he set a league record on defense by handling 573 straight chances without an error. The Mariners won 82 games and lost 80—not a great record, but satisfying for them.

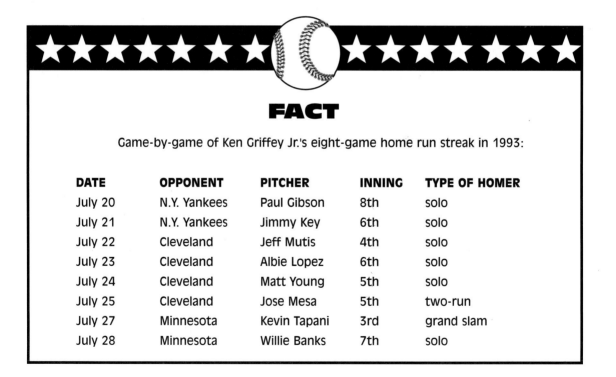

FACT

Game-by-game of Ken Griffey Jr.'s eight-game home run streak in 1993:

DATE	OPPONENT	PITCHER	INNING	TYPE OF HOMER
July 20	N.Y. Yankees	Paul Gibson	8th	solo
July 21	N.Y. Yankees	Jimmy Key	6th	solo
July 22	Cleveland	Jeff Mutis	4th	solo
July 23	Cleveland	Albie Lopez	6th	solo
July 24	Cleveland	Matt Young	5th	solo
July 25	Cleveland	Jose Mesa	5th	two-run
July 27	Minnesota	Kevin Tapani	3rd	grand slam
July 28	Minnesota	Willie Banks	7th	solo

The Man had arrived.

His swing was beautiful to watch. With his powerful left-handed stroke, few of his home runs barely cleared the fence. There was no suspense, no outfielder leaping at the warning track. When Griffey homered, the fielder stopped, stood, and watched the ball hit orbit.

By 1994, at the age of twenty-four, he was in his prime. Griffey was now the dominant player in baseball. He was setting the baseball world ablaze with his power, his athleticism, and—still—his youth. As the season unwound, Griffey flirted with history. He had 20 homers before the end of May. He hit number 30 off the California Angels' Brian Anderson ten days before the end of June. That snapped Babe Ruth's sixty-six-year record for most homers before June 30. Babe Ruth! Griffey was traveling in some pretty fast company.

Junior said that Ruth's record meant little to him. One record was important: In a May 23 game against the Oakland A's, Griffey belted his 21st homer of the season. That day, he passed his father's career total of 152. The goal now, he said, was to hit the most homers of any father-son combination in major-league history. "That would mean a lot to me," Junior told reporters. "It's something that no one can take away from us. If I don't break any other records, that one is something my dad and I can share."[5]

But it seemed possible by midseason that Griffey might break one of baseball's greatest all-time records—home runs in a season. Roger Maris had hit 61 back in 1961. Since then, no player had even come close.

In 1994, however, several players were taking a run at that record. In the National League, San Francisco Giants slugger Matt Williams was just one or two behind Junior throughout the season. In the American League, Frank Thomas of the Chicago White Sox was staying even, too. Breaking the home-run record would be one of baseball's biggest accomplishments.

The fans recognized Griffey's stardom. He received 6.1 million fan votes to start in the July All-Star Game. No player in baseball history had ever gotten so many votes. As he played in cities around the league, Junior got applause usually saved only for the favorite hometown players. In Kansas City, he got a standing ovation after hitting a homer against the Royals. In Milwaukee, five fans painted their chests and stood next to each other to spell out GO-JR! Home or road, he had indeed become the Man. Only a few superstar athletes, such as Joe Montana, Magic Johnson, and Wayne Gretzky, ever reached the point where they were favorites anywhere they went.

Junior does not have the body of the classic home-run hitter. He doesn't have the giant barrel chest of 250-pound Frank Thomas or the bulging biceps of Matt Williams. For that matter, Griffey doesn't have Babe Ruth's big gut, either. His bat speed is above average, but not great. "He does have something you can't teach," manager Lou Piniella said. "He shifts his weight better than anyone I've ever seen. When he swings, he's putting everything into it. He hits everyone—left-handers and right-handers. I would pay to see him. He's amazing."[6]

Griffey also is real. Unlike so many superstars who never seem happy, Griffey enjoys life. In 1994, he and his wife, Melissa, had their first child. They named him Trey Kenneth—Ken Griffey III. The Mariners' general manager, Woody Woodward, sent Trey a player's contract dated for 2012. Junior joked that it wasn't for enough money.

The season was going great, but it all came to an end on August 12. Baseball's players and owners had been fighting over how to divide the game's money. To most fans, the issues seemed stupid. Both sides, after all, were making millions of dollars. Because the players and owners could not settle

Ken Griffey, Jr., admires one of his home run clouts as it clears the fence. In 1994, Griffey, Jr., was threatening to break Roger Maris' single season home run record when a strike ended the season on August 12.

their differences, the players went on strike in August, and the season was canceled on September 14. For the first time in ninety years, there was no World Series.

Junior ended up with 40 homers in 111 games. Had he played a full season, he was on pace to hit 58. And, who knows? With a hot streak, he might have broken Maris's record.

The strike made the season wind up a disappointment, but there was hope that if the strike were settled, 1995 could mean great things for the Mariners. Griffey was now considered baseball's

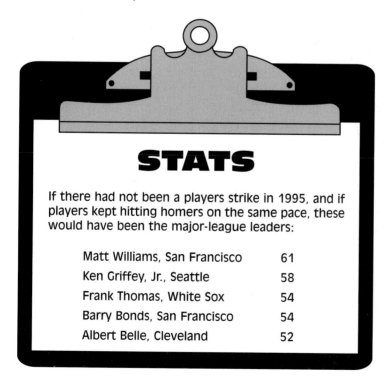

STATS

If there had not been a players strike in 1995, and if players kept hitting homers on the same pace, these would have been the major-league leaders:

Matt Williams, San Francisco	61
Ken Griffey, Jr., Seattle	58
Frank Thomas, White Sox	54
Barry Bonds, San Francisco	54
Albert Belle, Cleveland	52

premier player. The Mariners had built a strong team around him. It featured three other sluggers—outfielder Jay Buhner, first baseman Tino Martinez, and third baseman Edgar Martinez. Gigantic left-hander Randy Johnson was baseball's scariest pitcher.

Seattle's fans had never seen their team play in baseball's postseason. Would 1995 be the magic year?

Chapter 8

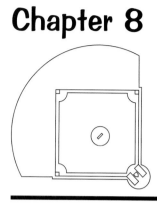

In the Playoffs

The 1995 season started out just fine. The Mariners won six of their first seven games. They spent the first month fighting for first place. Then disaster came.

On May 26, Junior made a spectacular catch to rob the Baltimore Orioles' Kevin Bass of an extra-base hit. In making the play, he crashed into the Kingdome fence. He broke two bones in his left wrist. The next day, doctors operated for three hours. They put seven screws and a metal plate inside his wrist to help it heal. They predicted he would miss three months.

Seattle's season seemed over before it had really started. But manager Lou Piniella told his players that they should "refuse to lose. We lost a big piece

Ken Griffey, Jr., will do all that he can to catch a ball, often risking serious injury. On May 26, 1995, Griffey crashed into the wall and broke his wrist after robbing Kevin Bass of an extra-base hit. The injury caused him to miss most of the season.

in Junior. But we've got players with plenty of ability to get us the pennant."[1]

Well, not exactly. The Mariners won 36 games and lost 37 with Junior out of the lineup. It wasn't terrible, but it wasn't what Piniella had hoped for. By mid-August, they were thirteen games behind the first-place California Angels. Five players were keeping them alive. Lefty Randy Johnson had become the top pitcher in the American League, and four Mariners were in the league's top 10 for runs batted in. They were first baseman Tino Martinez, third baseman Mike Blowers, right fielder Jay Buhner, and designated hitter Edgar Martinez.

Junior worked hard to heal his wrist. On August 15—two weeks earlier than expected—he returned to the lineup. The savior was back. If the Mariners were going to make the playoffs for the first time in their history, they had to start winning immediately.

That didn't happen. In fact, the team lost six of its first nine games after he came back. Piniella told the players they were spending too much time watching Junior and not enough time hustling. Griffey was still struggling to get his timing back.

Soon, however, things started to click. During a seven-game winning streak in September, Junior hit 4 homers and drove in 12 runs. Two weeks later, the

Mariners won seven of eight home games. They caught the Angels.

The biggest game of the regular season came September 24 against the New York Yankees. Despite Jay Buhner's first-inning grand slam, the Mariners trailed, 7–6, in the bottom of the ninth. With two outs, outfielder Vince Coleman drew a walk, and second baseman Joey Cora singled. That brought up Junior. On the first pitch, he walloped a 3-run homer to win the game. It was the first game-ending home run he had ever hit, he later said.

The regular season ended with the Mariners and Angels tied for first place in the American League West. They held a one-game special playoff in Seattle to decide the champion. On October 2, the Mariners won that contest, 9–1, before 52,356 joyous fans. Junior contributed a single and a double. For the first time in their nineteen-year history, the Mariners were division champs. They would now go on to the face the Yankees in the American League division playoffs.

Before that series, reporters asked Junior how he felt. He was still just twenty-five, they said. He had never played in the postseason. Was he nervous?

"Not at all," he said. "I spent my childhood watching my father do well in the playoffs and

Griffey celebrates his first game winning home run.

World Series. I think he taught me not to be nervous. When it's time to perform, I'll know what to do."[2]

He sure did. In the first playoff game of his life, Griffey hit 2 home runs, singled, and scored 3 times. But Seattle's pitching collapsed, and the team lost, 9–6. The second game lasted 15 innings and five hours. Griffey socked another home run, but again, the Mariners lost, 7–5.

In two games, Junior had 3 homers, 5 hits, and 5 runs batted in. His team, however, was down, two games to none. One more loss, and its good season would be over.

The Mariners and Yankees then moved across the country to Seattle. Griffey felt much better about his team's chances playing in front of fifty-six thousand loyal fans at the Kingdome. He was right. The Mariners won the next game, 7–4, behind Johnson's strong pitching.

Facing another do-or-die game the next day, the Mariners fell behind the Yankees, 5–0. But Seattle's Edgar Martinez hit a 3-run homer in the third inning and then a grand slam in the eighth. Junior added a home run of his own, his fourth of the series. That broke an American League playoff series record for home runs by one player. The Mariners won, 11–8.

Yankee Manager Buck Showalter said he did not need to be reminded of Griffey's talent. "He didn't catch us by surprise in any form or fashion," Showalter said. "You end up not being surprised by great athletes. Those people rise to the occasion."[3]

Could he rise to the occasion one more time? Whichever team won Game 5 of the Mariners-Yankees series would go on to face the Cleveland Indians for the American League pennant. It was the biggest game of Junior's career and the Mariners' history.

As it turned out, it was a terrific game. The Yankees, behind pitcher David Cone, led, 4–2, after seven innings. Junior made it 4–3 with a solo home run (his fifth!) in the eighth inning. The Mariners tied it up in the ninth, taking the game into extra innings.

In the top of the 11th inning, the Yankees took a one-run lead on a single by Randy Velarde. The Mariners came up in the bottom of the inning down 5–4 and—yet again—facing elimination. Joey Cora beat out a drag bunt, and Junior followed with a single up the middle. That brought up Edgar Martinez, who whacked a curveball into left field. It looked like it would score Cora to tie the game.

It did just that, but it did more, as well.

Junior flew from first base as Martinez hit the ball. He came streaming past second base like an Olympic sprinter. Third base coach Sam Perlozzo put up the sign for Griffey to stop at third, but Junior ignored the signal. He ran like crazy as Yankees outfielder Bernie Williams threw the ball in. As it was relayed to home, Junior slid into the plate.

Safe! He had scored the winning run on a mad dash. The Mariners had won the series. Junior was mobbed by his teammates. The fans at the Kingdome, many of them wearing Refuse to Lose shirts, roared.

"He was determined to score from the get-go," coach Perlozzo said in the postgame celebration. "He knew he had a chance, so why not go for it? It was risky, but he made it. That's as fast as I've seen Junior run in the three years I've been here."[4]

The win meant that the Mariners magical season was still alive. They now went on to play the Cleveland Indians. The tough Indians had won 100 games during the regular season—twenty-two more than Seattle. But the Mariners had won five of the nine games played between the two teams in 1995. Could they keep the edge?

For the first four games, the series was even. Junior had 4 hits in the games. Mostly, however, the two teams got by on their pitching. The series was tied, two games apiece.

In the fifth game, the Mariners trailed, 3–2, in the seventh inning. With runners on first and third and one out in the seventh, Griffey came up to face reliever Paul Assenmacher. Junior wanted to win the game and swung for the fences, but he struck out on four pitches. The Mariners lost. One more loss, and Cleveland would win the pennant.

On October 17, the Mariners again played for their lives. A crowd of 58,499 gave the team a standing ovation as it ran onto the Kingdome field. Seattle's Randy Johnson and Cleveland's Dennis Martinez engaged in a great pitchers' duel for seven innings. No one could score. In the eighth, Cleveland pushed 4 runs across the plate. The Mariners struggled to come back, but Martinez was too tough. The Indians won, 4–0.

Despite the loss, Mariners fans gave the team a standing ovation as the game ended. Most stayed in the stadium and kept cheering for ten minutes until Griffey led his teammates back onto the field for a final good-bye wave.

"It was a start, not an end," Junior said of the season. "It was a blast. This season is over, but I think we all got a taste of something we want more of. I always have fun playing baseball, but this season, the last month, was great for all of us. The team, the fans, the city. We'll be back."[5]

Junior could not wait to come back for the 1996 season. He was having another terrific year when he injured his right wrist in June. For the seventh straight year, baseball's fans elected him to start in the All-Star Game. Unfortunately, he was unable to play. He returned to Seattle's lineup midway through July.

There is no telling how great Ken Griffey Junior's career will turn out. At the age of twenty-six, when some players are still struggling to make the majors, his home run total has zipped past 200. He has it all—power, defense, speed, and baseball smarts.

During the 1997 season, Griffey, Jr. used all of his

STATS

Most Major-League Home Runs by Father-Son Combinations (up to the end of the 1997 season):

FATHER	HR	SON	HR	TOTAL
Bobby Bonds	332	Barry Bonds	374	706
Ken Griffey, Sr.	152	Ken Griffey, Jr.	294	446
Gus Bell	206	Buddy Bell	201	407
Yogi Berra	358	Dale Berra	49	407

Ken Griffey, Jr., has enormous talent and a love for the game that is possibly unmatched. This combination could make him one of the best and most exciting players in baseball history.

tools to help lead the Mariners to a first place finish in the AL's Western Division. Griffey, Jr., had an amazing season. He led the American League in home runs, runs batted in, and runs scored. All this was good enough to win him the AL MVP Award. The Mariners, however, were defeated in the Divisional Playoffs by the Baltimore Orioles, three games to one.

"I can't think of a better job than playing baseball," he once said. "It's a joy to play the game. My teammates are my best friends. And there is nothing better than pleasing the fans with a home run. If I could, I would play forever."[6]

Someday, when the names of the greatest baseball players of all time are called out, the list will include the familiar names: Babe Ruth. Willie Mays. Hank Aaron. Reggie Jackson. Cal Ripken, Jr.

Don't be surprised if the list also includes Ken Griffey, Jr.

Chapter Notes

Chapter 1

1. Bob Ryan, "In Awe of Griffey's Amazing Grace," *Boston Globe*, October 14, 1995, p. C1.

2. Peter Schmuck, "Mariners Set Sail for Pennant Series; 2-Run Double Knocks Out Yankees," *Baltimore Sun*, October 9, 1995, p. D1.

3. Bob Finnigan, "In the Aftermath, Mariners Tell Fans: 'We'll be Back,'" *Seattle Times*, October 18, 1995, p. D1.

4. Robert Markus, "Griffey gets High Marks in Heredity," *Chicago Tribune*, April 18, 1992, p. 1C.

5. Bob Sherwin, "Mariners' Griffey Set to Make Big Money, Not Big Change," *Philadelphia Inquirer*, October 4, 1992, p. D13.

6. Milton Kent, "A Young Star Rising Higher and Higher, Great Things Were Expected of Ken Griffey Junior," *Philadelphia Inquirer*, September 12, 1993, p. C3.

Chapter 2

1. Robert Markus, "Griffey gets High Marks in Heredity," *Chicago Tribune*, April 18, 1992, p. 1C.

2. Mark Maske, "Griffey Still Learning Role," *Washington Post*, September 1, 1993, p. 1D.

3. Jim Donaghy, "Baseball Sprouts Second Generation; Dads and Money Sons Can Make," *Philadelphia Inquirer*, April 18, 1990, p. 1D.

4. Mike Lupica, "Roger and Him," *Esquire*, September 1994, p. 67.

5. E. M. Swift, "Bringing Up Junior," *Sports Illustrated*, May 7, 1990, p. 42.

6. Hank Hersch, "Born to be a Major Leaguer," *Sports Illustrated*, May 16, 1988, p. 69.

Chapter 3

1. Jeff Schultz, "Griffey Hasn't Gotten Down to Business," *San Jose Mercury News*, June 6, 1988, p. 1C.

2. Bob Finnegan, "Griffey Jr. Reveals His '88 Suicide Attempt," *Philadelphia Daily News*, March 6, 1992, p. 70.

3. Ibid., p. 71.

4. Hank Hersch, "Born to be a Major Leaguer," *Sports Illustrated*, May 16, 1988, p. 68.

5. Ibid.

6. Schultz, p. 1C.

Chapter 4

1. Dan Shaughnessy, "Griffey Jr. Inherited Dad's Gift," *Charlotte Observer*, May 14, 1989, p. 3D.

2. Bud Geracie, "The Rookies: Griffey May Duel Sheffield," *San Jose Mercury News*, March 19, 1989, p. 1D.

3. Dan Hruby, "Following in His Dad's Footsteps," *San Jose Mercury News*, April 4, 1989, p. 5E.

4. Ibid.

5. Associated Press, "Griffey Jr. on Hitting Tear," *Wichita Eagle-Beacon*, April 28, 1989, p. 3D.

6. Associated Press, "Mariners' Griffey Sidelined by Broken Hand," *Lexington Herald-Leader*, July 26, 1989, p. D4.

Chapter 5

1. Ray Richardson, "Baseball Still a Playground for Maturing Youngster Griffey," *St. Paul Pioneer Press*, July 25, 1990, p. 4C.

2. M. G. Missanelli, "Hitting Stride—Curt and Cocky, Mariner Sails to Stardom," *Philadelphia Inquirer*, August 28, 1990, p. C1.

3. Ibid.

4. Charlie Vincent, "Griffey, Son Live a Dream," *Detroit Free Press*, September 26, 1990, p. 1D.

5. Associated Press, "Griffeys Make History and Drama," *Akron Beacon-Journal*, September 1, 1990, p. C1.

6. Vincent, p. 1D.

Chapter 6

1. Helene Elliott, "Critical Column Sparks Griffey, Young Outfielder Key to Franchise," *Los Angeles Times*, August 25, 1991, p. 5B.

2. Ibid.

3. Associated Press, "Griffey Jr. Shows Both Sides of His Fame Against Orioles," *Wichita Eagle*, August 1, 1991, p. 4B.

4. Jim Caple, "Griffey Is Star of Stars for AL," *Akron-Beacon Journal*, July 15, 1992, p. C1.

5. Bob Finnigan and Bob Sherwin, "Griffey Pondering Long-Term Options," *Seattle Times*, November 1, 1992, p. D7.

6. Associated Press, "Defensive Griffey Says He's Not Mariners' Top Dog," *St. Paul Pioneer Press*, August 14, 1992, p. 5C.

Chapter 7

1. Blaine Newnham, "Griffey Maturing as Power Hitter, Leader," *Seattle Times*, May 13, 1993, p. 5D.

2. Steve Kelley, "Griffey Jr. Falls Short of Clout 9," *Seattle Times*, July 13, 1993, p. 4D.

3. Associated Press, "Griffey's Homer Streak Hits Record-Tying Eight," *Miami Herald*, July 29, 1993, p. 1D.

4. Jim Caple, "Twins Won't Let Griffey Cut a Record," *Miami Herald*, July 31, 1993, p. 1D.

5. Gary Washburn, "Junior's Circuit Clouts Make Him Game's Marquee Player at Age 24," *Detroit Free Press*, July 13, 1994, p. 4C.

6. Pedro Gomez, "Homer Chase: Griffey Is in Pursuit of Maris, Ruth," *Miami Herald*, June 24, 1994, p. 1D.

Chapter 8

1. Bob Sherwin, "Forced to Fly Without Junior, Mariners Found They Had Wings," *Seattle Times*, October 2, 1995, p. D8.

2. Bob Finnigan, "At Long Last, Champions," *Seattle Times*, October 3, 1995, p. F1.

3. Bob Finnigan, "Griffey's Opening Act a Big Hit," *Seattle Times*, October 4, 1995, p. C8.

4. Bob Ryan, "In Awe of Griffey's Amazing Grace," *Boston Globe*, October 14, 1995, p. C1.

5. Bob Finnigan, "In the Aftermath, Mariners Tell Fans: 'We'll Be Back,'" *Seattle Times*, October 18, 1995, p. D1.

6. Sherwin, p. D8.

Career Statistics

YEAR	TEAM	G	AB	R	H	2B	3B	HR	RBI	AVG.	BB	SO	SB
1987	Bellingham*	54	182	43	57	9	1	14	40	.313	44	42	13
1988	San Bernardino*	58	219	50	74	13	3	11	42	.338	34	39	32
	Vermont*	17	61	10	17	5	1	2	10	.279	5	12	4
1989	Seattle	127	455	61	120	23	0	16	61	.264	44	83	16
1990	Seattle	155	597	91	179	28	7	22	80	.300	63	81	16
1991	Seattle	154	548	76	179	42	1	22	100	.327	71	82	18
1992	Seattle	142	565	83	174	39	4	27	103	.308	44	67	10
1993	Seattle	156	582	113	180	38	3	45	109	.309	96	91	17
1994	Seattle	111	433	94	140	24	4	40	90	.323	56	73	11
1995	Seattle	72	260	52	67	7	0	17	42	.258	52	53	4
1996	Seattle	140	545	125	165	26	2	49	140	.303	78	104	16
1997	Seattle	157	608	125	185	34	3	56	147	.304	76	121	15
MAJOR LEAGUE TOTALS		1,214	4,593	820	1,389	261	24	294	872	.302	580	755	123

*Minor League statistics not included in totals.

Where to Write
Ken Griffey, Jr.

Mr. Ken Griffey, Jr.
c/o Seattle Mariners
P.O. Box 4100
Seattle, WA 98104

Index

McCaskill, Kirk, 55–56
McDowell, Jack, 26
McGriff, Fred, 43
Milligan, Randy, 60
Minnesota Twins, 71, 73
Moeller High School, 22–26
Montana, Joe, 78
Morris, Jack, 71
Mussina, Mike, 26

N
New York Yankees, 8, 9, 20, 45,
    48–49, 86, 88–90

O
Oakland A's, 40, 77
Ohio State University, 24, 52
Oklahoma, University of, 23
Olson, Gregg, 47

P
Perlozzo, Sam, 89–90
Piazza, Mike, 11
Piniella, Lou, 68–69, 70, 79, 83, 85
Plummer, Bill, 62–63
Puckett, Kirby, 71

R
Reynolds, Harold, 54
Ripken, Cal, Jr., 94
Riverfront Stadium, 13, 19
Rocky, 65
Rookie League, 27
Ruth, Babe, 77, 79, 94

S
San Bernardino Spirit, 33
San Francisco Giants, 11, 78
Sanders, Deion, 20
Seattle Times, 59
Showalter, Buck, 88–89
Sports Illustrated, 33
Star Wars, 65
Steib, Dave, 43
Stewart, Dave, 40
Strawberry, Darryl, 33
Sweet, Rick, 29

T
Tapani, Kevin, 73
Texas Rangers, 72
Thomas, Frank, 11, 78, 79
Toronto Blue Jays, 43, 44, 71
Trammell, Alan, 59

V
Vaughn, Mo, 11
Velarde, Randy, 89

W
Wells, David, 43
Williams, Bernie, 90
Williams, Matt, 78, 79
Winfield, Dave, 11
Woodward, Woody, 79
World Series, 19, 39, 62, 66, 81

Y
Yankee Stadium, 73